SHUT UP
AND FEEL

AN ADULT PICTURE BOOK ON EMOTIONS

DJ CORCHIN   DAN DOUGHERTY

the
phazelFoz
company, llc

Sometimes you get angry and you try to talk yourself into all the reasons why you shouldn't be angry.

Fuck that. Shut up and feel.

Rage.
Flip a table.

A big-ass pumpkin hurled at concrete...

...will definitely make you feel better.

Sometimes you feel depressed and people try to cheer you up.

Fuck that.

It's okay to bawl your eyes out.
Put on a sad song and sing along
at the top of your lungs
like it was your life being
described.

Paint fifty paintings in different shades of blue and then put on an art show called "My Pain."

Watch sad movies on repeat for 24 hours.

Blow up balloons and then pop them.
Aggressively.
Just shut up and feel.

Even the asshats who portray their perfect life on social media are doing it.
No one's that perfect.

Except Beyoncé. Beyoncé is perfect.

Aren't you Beyoncé?

Yes you are my little precious.
Who's a good kitty?

And don't hold back. Tell your therapist everything. I mean EVERYTHING. Like that time you took medicine to make yourself constipated just so you could feel something different.

Or the time you ate an entire cake because you FUCKING WANTED to! Not healthy, but once in a while you just need to eat your damn feelings.

Like jealousy.
Eat the hell out of jealousy.
It tastes so delicious.
It tastes like if frosting and cookie dough had a
baby after a three-way with a pumpkin spice latte.
Just shut up and feel.

Sometimes you feel anxious.
Like really anxious.

Like so anxious the
anti-diarrheal medicine
you took earlier has
no chance of working.

Allergic to cats? Hug a pillow. Oh and buy yourself one of those fucking huge pillows you can koala your legs around. It feels good.
Too good sometimes.

Need medication? If they're right for you, good! They can fucking work.

They're like a light switch in your head that tells your body, "fucking chill... you're okay."

And that dumbass influencer on social media who tells you medication is bad and you should try a nice spinach-banana colonic instead, is a fucking idiot. But you... you're gonna be just fine.

Sometimes your employer doesn't provide time off for mental health days. Fuck that.

Tell them you're taking a project management course and need the day to get certified.

If your "loved ones" think feeling is weak.
Fuck that.
Leave them alone. Get better. Then show them how fucking awesome feeling is by becoming the best version of yourself WITH your emotions, not in spite of them.

Then refer that "loved one" back to page twenty-six where they'll learn about eating jealousy and three-ways with a coffee drink.

We are human.
YOU are human.
Humans feel.
Humans feel good and humans feel bad.

But they FEEL.
They feel SO MANY THINGS!

So the next time you sense your insides creating a fusion reaction or tears are about to spray from your face uncontrollably, know you're human, you're good, and you will be alright.

But for fuck's sake, most of all... shut up and feel.

Dedicated to ourselves. We're fucking awesome.
You are too.
In fact, this book is also dedicated to you.
We can dedicate it to more people.
It's our fucking book.

– DJ & Dan

This book is not intended as professional advice. It is strictly for entertainment purposes. Please seek help from a mental health professional and know that you are loved and not alone.

Published by The phazelFOZ Company, LLC. Oak Park, IL
www.phazelfoz.com
Library of Congress Number: 2023938274

ISBN 978-1-7328646-2-7 (Hardcover)